Surfing a perfect, clean-breaking wave is an amazing feeling. The Hawaiian kings began surfing hundreds of years ago. People enjoy it just as much today.

Surfers have always lived a free life, following the seasons and swells, in search of perfect waves.

types of surfing

There are many ways of riding waves. Each type of surfing has its own different style. But all surfers need one thing – a well-shaped wave.

Body surfing
This is where you use your body to catch the wave. You often wear flippers on your feet.

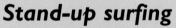

Body boarding
Body boarders ride a plastic board lying on their stomachs.

Stand-up surfing
This is the real thing. It is the most difficult to do, but also the most exciting.

Other types of surfing
Sea canoeing and wave skiing.
The canoes and skis are moved using paddles. The rider sits down when surfing.

Kneeboarding means riding a fibreglass board on your knees. A kneeboard is like a real surfboard but shorter and wider.

waves

There are many different types of wave to be found in the oceans.

Beach break

This is the most common type of wave, found on beaches. Most people learn on beach breaks because they are easier and safer to ride.

Point break

These are usually found by headlands. The waves can be long and great to ride but there are often rocks below.

Tim Rainger

Tim Rainger

Reef break

Many of the world's most famous waves break over reefs. The reefs are covered by shallow water. They are often the most dangerous spots. There are rock and coral reefs in every ocean.

7

safety

Surfing big waves is dangerous. Surfing small waves can also be dangerous for many reasons. Always remember that the ocean is much more powerful than us.

You need to be a strong swimmer. You also need to learn about the ocean and how to spot dangers such as –

- **rips (fast-moving ocean currents)**
- **rocks**
- **freak waves**
- **changing tides.**

All can be killers.

The sun

The water reflects the sun and many surfers have good tans. But skin cancer can be a big problem. Always use sun block when you go surfing.

Ocean life

There are some dangerous creatures in the ocean – like sharks, jellyfish and sea urchins. You should also try to avoid sewage or other pollution.

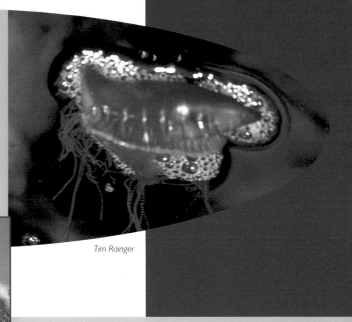

Tim Rainger

Wipeouts

Wiping out means falling off. You should try to avoid landing on your board when you fall.

Crowds

Crashing into other surfers is a big hassle. When you're learning it's best not to go out when it's crowded.

the board

Most surfboards are handmade from foam and fibreglass. They are light and quite strong. They come in many shapes and sizes to suit things like your weight and how good a surfer you are.

Most boards have three fins. Boards with three fins are called 'thrusters'. The fins help to stop your board sliding sideways.

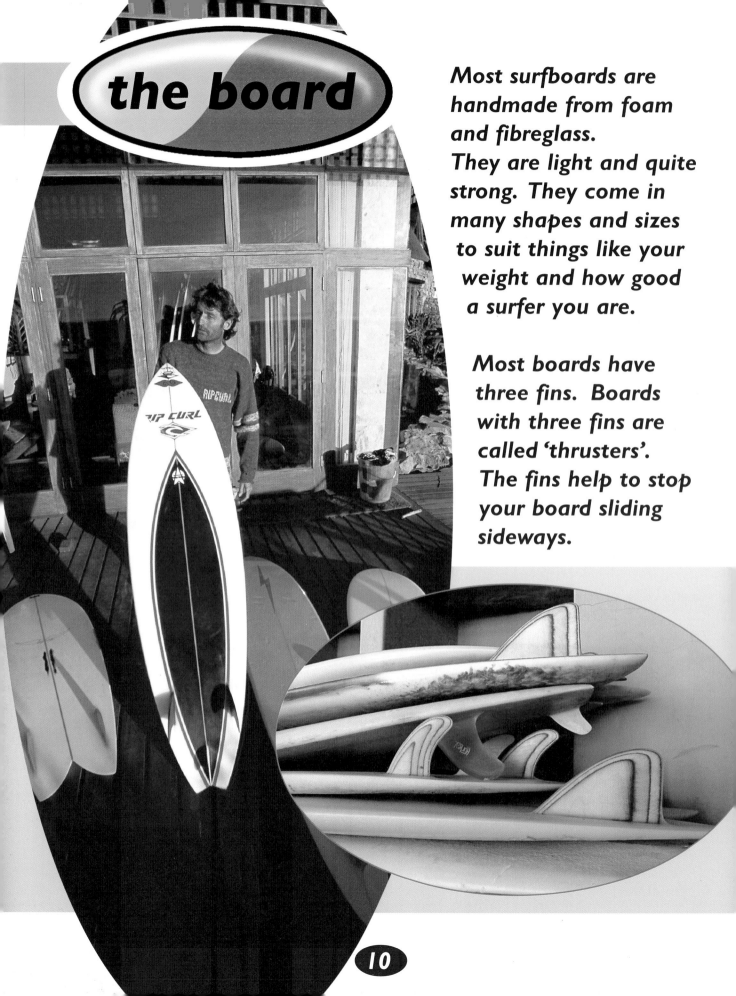

Buying your first board

It's best to try a few different length boards before you buy. Find out what's best for you. Go to a good surf shop. Be honest with them about how good a surfer you are and they'll help you out.

types of surfboard

Pics above:
S.Cazenave-Nikon

The longboard or malibu

The original Hawaiian surfers rode very long boards without fins. Malibus were the first boards with fins. They are nearly three metres long and quite wide and thick. They are very good to learn on and great fun in small surf.

Shortboards

These are lightweight boards for more experienced riders. They are usually about two metres long. Most of the boards you'll see are shortboards.

Guns

These are boards for big waves. They are long and thin.

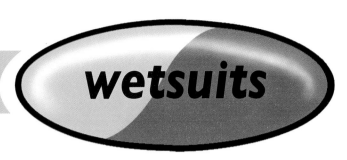

wetsuits

Wetsuits are made of a special rubber. They come in different thicknesses and cuts. There are different suits for different types of weather. In winter you'll need a full suit, called a steamer, and often booties as well. In cold countries you'll probably need a rubber hood and gloves. In warmer countries you can get away without a suit for much of the time.

Types of wetsuit

- Steamer. This type of wetsuit has long legs and long arms.
- Short-sleeve steamer. These have long legs and short arms.
- Spring suit. These have short legs and short arms.
- A short john has short legs and no arms.

There are two main types of stitching used in wetsuits.

- Blind stitched suits. These suits are usually glued and only let some water in.
- Overlocked suits. These are not watertight and usually leak through the seams.

Tim Rainger

Thickness

Wetsuits are often referred to by the thickness of the rubber. For example, a 5/4/3 is 5 millimetres (mm) thick around the body, 4mm around the legs, and 3mm around the arms.

Fit

Wetsuits should fit snugly but not too tightly. Avoid suits with a very tight neck. Very loose suits can give you a bad rash as they will rub under your arms. To stop this, use a rash vest (see page 17).

clothing and accessories

Leash

This is a rubber cord which attaches you to the board. Bodyboarders tie the leash to their wrists, stand-up surfers to their ankles. When you lose control of your board, the leash makes sure you don't have to swim for miles to get it back or even lose it completely.

Wax or deck grip

Water will make your surfboard slippery. To get a good grip you can use wax. Rub it slowly onto the deck (top) of your board on the places where you stand. It does come off, so you have to 'wax up' often.

Some people use rubber deck grip which sticks to the board and never comes off.

Clothing

Surf clothing has always been baggy and comfortable. The main thing you need is a pair of boardshorts. These dry quickly and usually have a fixed waist – so they don't come off!

Tim Rainger

If you're wearing a wetsuit, you'll probably need a lycra shirt underneath. They are known as rash vests or rashies. They will stop you getting rashes under your arms from paddling.

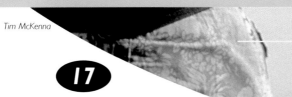

Tim McKenna

getting started

Paddling

To surf, you first have to learn how to paddle. Lie on the board so that it is balanced. Your face should be about three-quarters of the way up the board. Start swimming with your hands. You can practise paddling without waves.

Tim Ranger

Where to go

You must then decide when and where to go out surfing. This will depend on things like the size of the waves and the direction of the wind and tide. Watch the surf for a few minutes before choosing somewhere that's easy to paddle out to.

Paddle out

Attach the leash to your ankle at the water's edge. Walk in until you're up to your waist. If you start paddling before it's deep enough you may damage your board. Then paddle as hard as you can until you are past where the waves are breaking. This is known as 'getting out the back'.

up and riding

Standing up

Once you're out the back, face the shore and wait until you see a wave form. Start paddling before it comes to you. Keep paddling as it begins to pick you up, then jump to your feet. Stand with your knees bent and your back foot over the back fin.

Goofy or natural?

Some people stand with their left foot forward (natural) and some with their right foot (goofy). Find out which one feels most comfortable.

Riding the whitewater
Most beginners learn by riding the whitewater after a wave has broken. You just go in a straight line, but it's a good way to get used to being on a board.

The power pocket
The closer you ride to 'the curl' (or 'the lip') of a breaking wave, the more power and speed you will get. This part of the wave is known as the 'power pocket'. It may take you many attempts to get in the power pocket.

moves

Once you feel happy standing on your board you'll want to go on to try something more difficult. Over the next few pages we'll look at some of the moves. Look at the pictures to get some tips. But remember that the only real way to learn is to keep practising.

Take off

The first thing to learn is how to get to your feet. When you feel the wave begin to carry you, push up with your hands and spring to your feet.

Bottom turn

The first real turn a surfer learns is the bottom turn. After taking off, you turn at the bottom of the wave to bring you face-to-face with it.

Cut back

When you go faster than the breaking wave, you must turn your board to 'cut back' to the power pocket. Otherwise, you will lose speed and stop.

Re-entry

A re-entry is any move where you turn your board back into the wave after you have left it.

tube riding

and aerials

Tube riding (or 'getting barrelled')
This is when the wave breaks over your head and it feels like you are riding inside a tube of water. It is one of the biggest thrills for any surfer.

Aerials

Aerials are about getting into the air. They are the most spectacular tricks in surfing.

big waves

Big wave riding is the ultimate test for any surfer. It is dangerous and any mistake you make could be your last.

searching

for the perfect wave

Most of the planet's surface is made up of water.
There will always be good waves somewhere in the oceans.
You can also find waves in some big lakes and rivers.

The Pacific Ocean has thousands of miles of great waves on its beaches and islands. Countries like Australia, the USA, New Zealand and all of South America have superb surf for much of the year. Hawaii has the biggest waves in the world.

The coastline of the Indian Ocean has excellent waves. This includes places like West Australia, Indonesia, South Africa and many others.

B. Sutherland

The Atlantic Ocean is not as well-known by surfers. But it has excellent waves on the coasts of Europe, Eastern USA, North Africa and the Atlantic Islands (like the Canaries). It's colder than the Indian and the Pacific but still good.

Eric Chauché

As long as you can get to a coast, you will find waves. Go for it!

Tim Rainger

extra stuff

First published in 1998 by Franklin Watts
© Franklin Watts 1998

Franklin Watts, 96 Leonard Street
London EC2A 4RH

Franklin Watts Australia, 14 Mars Road
Lane Cove NSW 2066

A CIP catalogue for this book is
available from the British Library.
ISBN 0 7496 3045 0 (Hardback)
      0 7496 3614 9 (Paperback)
Dewey classification: 797.3
Printed in Great Britain

Text: Tim Rainger
Photos: Alex Williams (except where indicated)
Series editor: Matthew Parselle
Art director: Robert Walster
Designer: Andy Stagg
Reading consultant: Frances James

Disclaimer: In the preparation of this book all
due care has been exercised with regard to
the activities depicted. The Publishers regret
that they can accept no liability for any loss or
injury sustained.

For more information contact:
Low Pressure, Tel 0181 9601 916
Surf Life Saving Inc (Australia),
Tel 02 9729 0212

Index